The Basketball Defense Guide

by   Sidney Goldstein

author of **The Basketball Coach's Bible**

and **The Basketball Player's Bible**

GOLDEN AURA PUBLISHING

The Nitty-Gritty Basketball Series

The Basketball Defense Guide
by Sidney Goldstein

Published by:

GOLDEN AURA PUBLISHING

Post Office Box 41012

Philadelphia, PA 19127 U.S.A.

Second Edition Copyright © 1999 by Sidney Goldstein
Printed in the U.S.A.

Library of Congress Card Number   98- 75673

Goldstein, Sidney

The Basketball Defense Guide

Sidney Goldstein.--Second Edition, 1999

Basketball-Coaching

ISBN 1-884357-33-4

Softcover

Contents

Introduction

Over many years of coaching, planning, and studying, I found ways to teach each and every skill even to the most unskilled player. This scheme of learning did not come from any book. I tried things in practice. I modified them till they worked. Even players who could not simultaneously chew bubble gum and walk learned the skills. This booklet, part of **The Nitty-Gritty Basketball Series**, is one result of this effort. I believe you can benefit from my work.

Who Can Use This Information

This booklet is the perfect tool for anybody who wants to coach, teach, and/or learn basketball:

- A parent who wants to teach his or her child
- A player who wants to understand and play the game better
- A little league or recreation league coach
- A high school or junior high school coach
- A college coach, a professional coach
- A women's or a men's coach

This booklet contains material from **The Basketball Player's Bible**. Chapter 1 gives the keys to learning the skills presented. I present the skills in lesson form. Chapter 2 gives the features of each lesson. The largest chapter, Chapter 3, presents the lessons in order. Check the **Lessons Needed Before** feature as you progress.

This guide contains 3 rebounding lessons along with the defensive lessons. The rebounding lessons teach boxing out, another defensive skill. **The Basketball Player's Bible** contains these lessons and many other related ones.

Golden Aura's Nitty-Gritty Basketball Series
by Sidney Goldstein

See the description in the back of this book.

The Basketball Coach's Bible

The Basketball Player's Bible

The Basketball Shooting Guide

The Basketball Scoring Guide

The Basketball Dribbling Guide

The Basketball Defense Guide

The Basketball Pass Cut Catch Guide

Basketball Fundamentals

Planning Basketball Practice

Videos for the Guides soon available

HOW TO CONTACT THE AUTHOR

The author seeks your comments about this book. Sidney Goldstein is available for consultation and clinics with coaches and players. Contact him at:

Golden Aura Publishing
PO Box 41012
Philadelphia, PA 19127
215 438-4459

Chapter One

1

Principles of Learning

How To Use The Defense Guide

Start from the beginning and progress through the lessons one by one. Typically, I arrange them in order of increasing difficulty. You may want to skip some topics. However, use the **Lessons Needed Before** feature to insure that you do not omit needed techniques.

The most important as well as the most frequently skipped lessons involve techniques. If you spend the needed time on these lessons, you will improve exponentially on a daily basis. Skip them and improvement may be delayed for months and even years.

One big misconception about learning the basics is that to improve you must practice things millions of times. I've tried it and so has everybody else. It does not work well. Volume of practice does not necessarily bring about improvement; practicing properly insures improvement. The following **principles** tell you what and how to practice. A list of **Counterproductive Beliefs** follows. These often widely held ideas prevent learning because they do not work.

The Principles of Defense

1. You need to be in a body position than enables you to move quickly as well as maintain this position while moving. See Lessons 1-2.

2. You need to stay with and move with the offensive player. See Lessons 2-11 except 9.

3. Always force the offense to one side or the other whether or not they have the ball. See Lessons 3-6 and 10.

4. You also must prevent low post players from moving where they want to go. It is easy to box out if you play defense properly. See Lessons 6-8.

5. Defensing the pick can be tricky. It requires lots of communication and experience. See Lesson 11.

6. Proper strong and weak side defense is the key to effective team defense. Weak side defenders must help out on the ball. See Lessons 7-9.

7. Hustle is a big part of defense. Lessons 2-7 teach this.

Counterproductive Beliefs

1. Learning *on ball* defense is more important than *off ball* defense. Nope–both are of nearly equal importance. *Off ball* defense is probably more important, because four players are off the ball at any moment. One-on-one any offensive player can go around the defense. So, *off ball* players always need to help out. *Off ball* players must be in position to rebound as well.

2. Defense is difficult to learn. Nope. Defense is much easier to learn than any offensive skill. Less skill is involved. A player can become expert in weeks rather than the months or years it takes for offense.

3. You can't teach hustle. Nope. It is one of the easiest, if not the easiest, skill to teach. All of the players I ever coached hustled.

The Principles of Rebounding

1. Rebounding involves pivoting, so you need to be an expert before you start.

2. Rebounding involves grabbing and pulling the ball away as well as pivoting.

3. One key to rebounding, which is often skipped, is predicting where the ball will go. You need to watch shot arcs carefully.

4. You need to be ready, in the ready position, for errant bounces and loose balls especially in a foul shooting situation. See Lesson 12.

5. You need to go for offensive and defensive rebounds in a similar way. Positioning and boxing out are keys. Lessons 13 and 14 teach boxing out starting from different situations.

Counterproductive Beliefs

1. You need to be tall and have a 4-foot vertical jump to rebound well. Not necessarily true. These attributes help, but smarts will help just as much. Some players always seem to be around the ball even though they are short or can barely jump. These lessons make you smarter.

2. Rebounding involves just going for the ball. Not so. Good rebounders do the following things:

•Watch shot arcs and the shooter; predict where the ball will go; get position on the opponent; rarely get boxed out; often come from behind the basket.

Chapter Two

2

Lesson Features

Table Information

At a glance this table gives an overview to aid in planning. It supplies the name and number of each lesson as well as these additional features: lessons needed before, the number of players needed, the effort level, the estimated practice times, whether you need a ball and/or a court. Practice the *no ball* or *no court* lessons for homework while watching TV or sitting down. The Player's Corner section of each lesson supplies some of the same information.

Number

The lessons are numbered in order from easiest to hardest, from most fundamental to most complicated. Typically, do them in order. Sometimes you can skip. If you do, check the **Lessons Needed Before** feature so that you do not skip essential lessons.

Name

A name related to each lesson serves as a descriptive mnemonic device (I almost forgot that). When skills are executed simultaneously, their names are directly coupled like Pivot Around Shoot or Jump Hook. Lessons with skills separately performed are named, for example, Pivot with Defense, where one player pivots on offense while the other is on defense.

Brief

In one sentence (usually) the **brief** immediately familiarizes you with the lesson by stating the action and movement involved.

Why Do This

When do you use this in a game? What is the significance of the lesson? What fundamentals do you practice? How does this lesson relate to others? The **Why Do This** section answers these questions.

Directions

These are step-by-step directions for you.

Key Points

This feature emphasizes important points in the directions so that you will not make common mistakes.

When You Are More Expert

These more expert lessons usually add another step, combine another skill, or change one variable in the previous lesson. Some lessons have as many as four expert additions.

Player's Corner and Section Tables

At a glance you can see that the **Player's Corner** lists 8 useful pieces of information about each lesson. The **Table of Lessons** in **Appendix C** and each **Section Table** contain this same information. **Xs** in the tables mean <u>yes</u>. Dashes (-) mean <u>no</u>.

• Lessons Needed Before

Do these lessons before this current one. If you don't, then you will have a problem. Often you can skip lessons without it being disastrous. Not so with the lessons listed as Lessons Needed Before.

• Additional Needs

This feature gives 4 useful pieces of information.

Ball and Court

For most lessons you need a **ball** and a **court**. However, for some either one or the other or both are not needed. These lessons can be practiced at home while watching TV or in your backyard. **Xs** in the tables mean <u>yes</u>.

Players

Most lessons are for individuals. So, the Player's Corner lists additional players needed, whereas the Tables give the total number (which is always one more than additional players).

Assist

For some lessons you need an inactive **assistant** to either act as a dummy player or more importantly to closely watch what you are doing. **Xs** in the tables mean <u>yes</u>.

• Effort or Effort Level

The effort level of a lesson involves the physical effort involved. Level 1 lessons involve technique. Do them slowly;

they often do not resemble the skill performed in a game because 2 to 5 technique lessons often comprise a skill. In situations calling for defense, the defense expends little effort.

Level 2 lessons are at the practice level. Any skill practiced at a moderate pace like shooting or pivoting is at level 2. This level is a catchall for lessons between levels 1 and 3. Defense against offense makes a moderate effort.

Level 3 lessons are at the game level. Players sprint and perform at maximum effort. Pressure is on players. Offense and defense go full speed against each other. Games are easy compared to these lessons.

• Daily Practice Time

This is a time range needed to practice this lesson. Note that many lessons have additional parts. These will take more time.

• More Expert Lessons

Each of these additions adds one or two parameters to the main lesson. Few are optional. Most need to be done after you are more expert.

FEATURES OF THE DIAGRAMS

Lines and Arrows

Solid lines indicate movement of players whereas dashed lines usually indicate movement of the ball. One exception is dashed lines used to show pivoting direction. The types of arrows used are solid for movement and hollow for passes. A different type of arrow head is used for fakes. See the diagrams.

Body Position of Player

The body of a player is shown from an overhead view two ways. The line or the ellipse represents the shoulders. The

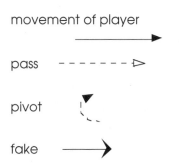

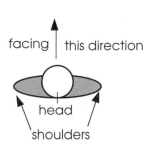

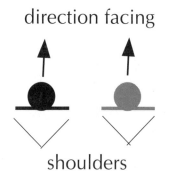

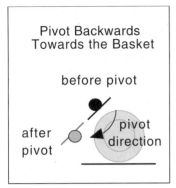

Pivot Backwards
Towards the Basket

before pivot

after pivot

pivot direction

circle shows the head. The player is always facing away from the shoulders toward the head.

Shades for Different Positions

When a player is shown in two positions in the same diagram, the first position is black and the second is lighter in color. Often offense or defense are shown in light and dark shades. In some diagrams shades are used to designate the position of a player when the ball of the same shade is in the diagramed position.

Numbers in Multistep Movements

Many drills involve multiple steps. Each step, as well, may have several timed movements that need to be executed in order. So, in the diagrams for each step, the numbers indicate the order of the movements. One (1) means first, two (2) second and so on. If two players move at the same time the numbers will be the same, so there may be several ones or twos in the diagram.

In the diagram below, there are three ones in the diagram. This indicates that these players move at the same time. There are two twos; one indicates a cut, while the other indicates a pass.

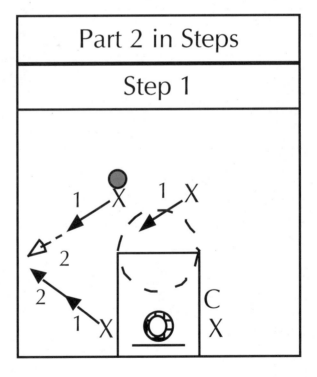

Part 2 in Steps

Step 1

Chapter Three

3

Defense and Rebound Lessons 1-14

L E S S O N	NAME	A S S I S T	P L A Y E R S	C O U R T	B A L L	E F F O R T	L E S S O N	Lessons Before	REF TO *Coach's Manual*	DAILY TIME	E X T R A
1-14	**DEFENSE and REBOUND**										
1	Defensive Position	-	1	-	-	1	1	none	12.0	2-4	0
2	Move in D Position 1-3	-	1	-	-	1-3	2	1	12.1	5-25	0
3	Force Left & Right1-5	x	2	-	-	1-2	3	2	12.2	2-5@	0
4	Three Yard Lesson	x	2	-	-	2-3	4	3	12.21	5-15	1
5	Trapping 1-3	-	3	-	-	2-3	5	4	12.3	10-15	1
6	Front Keep Out of Lane	-	2	x	-	3	6	2	12.4	10-15	1
7	Overplaying 1-6	-	2	x	-	1-3	7	4	12.5	10-20@	0
8	Defense the Low Post 1-3	x	2+	x	-	1-2	8	7	12.6,17.0	10-15	1
9	D on Shooter	x	2	x	x	2	9	5	12.7	3-8	1
10	D on Driver	-	2	x	x	2-3	10	9	12.71	5-10	1
11	Defensing the Pick 1-2	x	4	x	x	2	11	10	13.01	10-20	0
12	Rebound Ready Position	x	1	x	x	1-2	12	none	11.11	1	1
13	Step in Front Box Out 1-2	x	2	x	x	3	13	12	11.2	5-10	1
14	Block Box Out 1-2	-	2	x	x	2-3	14	12	11.3	10-20	0

1 Defensive Position

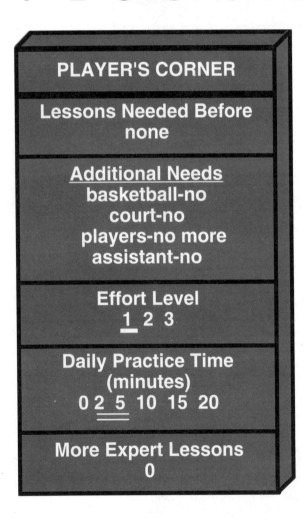

Brief:

This lesson describes the basic defensive body position.

Why Do This

The easiest skills to learn are the defensive skills. Unlike offensive ones like shooting and dribbling, which require adroitness, defensive skills require mostly sweat. You will master defensive lessons quickly and learn hustle as well. In addition, the defensive position is very similar to the dribbling position. It is no coincidence that good dribblers are also good defensive players (the reverse need not be true). Practicing one accrues benefits to the other. Defensive lessons also improve conditioning.

The defensive body position is designed so that you can readily sprint in any direction. With slight modification you can tailor it to any defensive situation.

Directions

1. Start in the half down body position.

2. The feet are slightly more than shoulder width apart.

3. Put the right foot forward and rotate the left foot slightly (30-45 degrees) to the left.

up   half down   full down

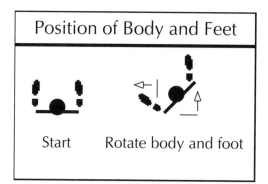

Position of Body and Feet

Start   Rotate body and foot

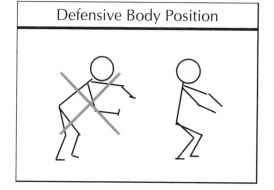

Defensive Body Position

4. Extend the right hand forward and slightly upward to block the pass and the view of the offense. The palm faces the defense; the fingers are fully separated, clawed and stretched upward.

5. Extend the left hand sideways, low to the ground, to cover the ball. The fingers are clawed and point downward.

6. Body weight is on the ball of each foot. You are now in the defensive body position.

7. Tap dance by moving each foot one inch off the ground. This looks like a football drill. With each tap count out loud by ones up to 20.

8. Put the left foot forward and switch arm positions. Put the right arm down, the left arm up. Repeat steps 1-7.

9. Continue until you are comfortable.

Key Points

1. The knees are bent, not the back. If your back is bent, do this lesson in the full down position.

2. The hand of the forward foot is up to block the pass; the hand of the back foot is down to cover the dribble.

3. Body weight is on the balls of the feet.

4. The quicker the tap dance, the better.

2 Move in D Position 1-3

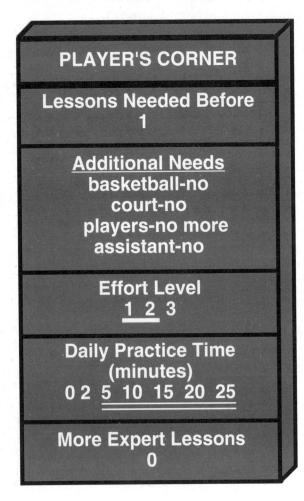

PLAYER'S CORNER

Lessons Needed Before
1

Additional Needs
basketball-no
court-no
players-no more
assistant-no

Effort Level
<u>1 2</u> 3

Daily Practice Time
(minutes)
0 2 <u>5 10 15 20 25</u>

More Expert Lessons
0

Brief:
First you walk, then jog, then sprint in each direction from the defensive position.

Why Do This
Defensive movement starts from the defensive position practiced in Lesson 61. With a pivot and slight rotation of the hips, a player is able to quickly sprint in any direction. As with all defensive lessons this one involves hustle, dribbling position, and conditioning.

Directions

Part 1– Move Forward and Back

1. Start in the defensive position. Tap dance counting to 20.

2. Take 4 steps in the direction indicated– forward, back, left, right– following the instructions.

3. The first step is always a push off step in the opposite direction. Initially walk through the directions. See the diagrams.

4. Start with the right foot forward. To go forward push off with the back foot (step 1), take one step forward with the right foot (step 2), step with the left foot (step 3), and then the right (step 4).

5. Repeat this 2 more times. Repeat again with the left foot forward (3 times). Push off with the back foot, which is the right foot this time.

6. To go backward, push off with front foot (1), swivel the body to face backward, step with back foot (2) (after swiveling it is the forward foot) , then with the right (3), and then the left (4). Swivel forward again. Repeat this 2 more times. Then repeat 3 times with the left foot forward.

7. Combine the forward and backward movements. Move alternatively left and then right.

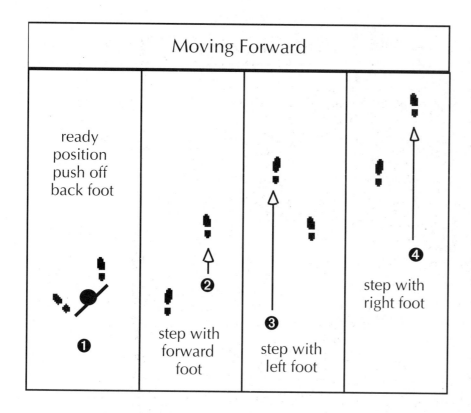

Moving Forward

ready position push off back foot ❶

step with forward foot ❷

step with left foot ❸

step with right foot ❹

Then go twice left and then twice right. When you can execute this at a fast pace, continue.

Part 2 Move Left and Right

8. Start with the right foot forward. To move left push off with the front right foot (1), step to the left with the left (2), step over with the right (3), and then the left (4).

Repeat this 2 more times. Then repeat with the left foot forward.

9. Start with the right foot forward. To move right push off with the back left foot (1), step right with the right (2), step in front with the left foot (3), and then with the right (4).

10. Repeat this 2 more times. Then repeat 3 times with the left foot forward.

11. Repeat the left and right movements alternatively speeding up the movements.

Part 3

12. Combine all movements—left, right, forward, and back—when ready. Tap dance in place between movements.

13. Here is a combined routine:

a. Right foot forward. Move forward, back, right, left.

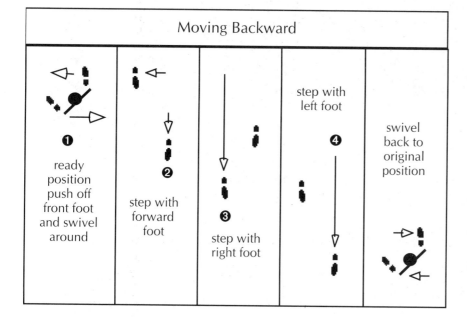

Moving Backward

ready position push off front foot and swivel around ❶

step with forward foot ❷

step with right foot ❸

step with left foot ❹

swivel back to original position

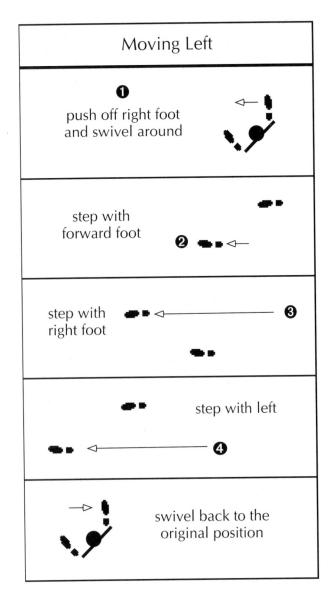

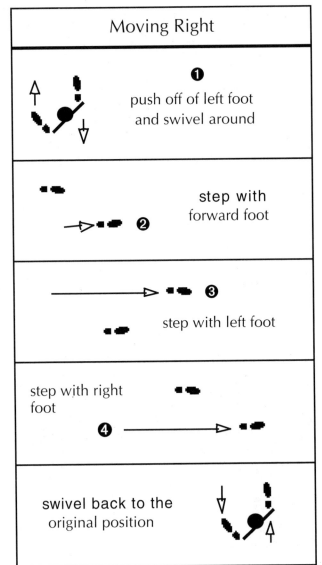

b. Repeat with the left forward.

c. Repeat **a** and **b** moving twice in each direction.

b. Repeat **a** and **b** moving in a different sequence like backward, right, forward, left, or reverse this.

14. Better yet, have an assistant call out the direction of motion. Make sure an assistant routinely instructs you to shift the forward foot.

Key Points

1. Remain in the half down position during this lesson.

2. Increase speed of execution slowly.

3. Tap dance between movements.

4. Find an assistant to call out the direction of motion when you are more expert.

3 Force Left & Right 1-5

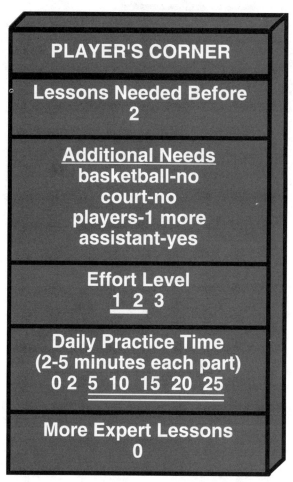

PLAYER'S CORNER

Lessons Needed Before
2

Additional Needs
basketball-no
court-no
players-1 more
assistant-yes

Effort Level
1 **2** 3

Daily Practice Time
(2-5 minutes each part)
0 2 5 10 15 20 25

More Expert Lessons
0

Brief:
The defense stays a constant distance from the offense, forcing them to dribble left or right.

Why Do This
The key to defensing a player with the ball is to stay a constant distance away depending on the offense's position. As the offense moves closer to the basket this distance decreases. Three yards is used for most lessons because at this distance you can easily recover from a mistake. You can readily shorten this distance for tighter coverage.

Most right handers prefer to dribble with the right hand, few like to use the left; lefties prefer to dribble with the left hand. Positioning the defense slightly to the right of a player forces the offense to both move and dribble left. See the diagram. Positioning to the left forces a player right. Forcing makes it more difficult for the offense to dribble up court, drive to the basket, or execute any ball movement. Forcing often hampers novices from dribbling.

This lesson has 5 parts.

Directions

Part 1

1. The defense sets up in defensive position, left foot forward, one foot away from the offense. See the diagram. Place your left foot one foot to the left of the offense. You are on the right of the offense. Offense, raise your right hand to convince doubters. If the offense goes right they bump into you. If they go left it is clear sailing. This is the *force left* position.

2. The *force right* position occurs when the right foot is forward, one foot right of the defense. Switch to the force right position.

3. Tap dance on the balls of the feet while switching back and forth several times.

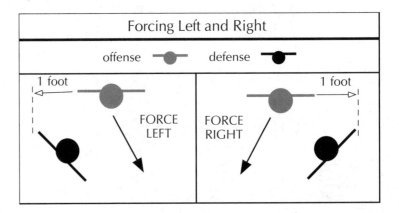

Part 2

4. Tap dance in the force left position. Back off 3 yards from the offense. Move 1 yard, then 2, then 3, and back again until you can estimate well.

5. The offense walks forward slowly for 2-4 seconds. The defense continues to maintain the 3 yard distance by jump stepping or sliding backward. Take small quick steps. When you take a jump step do not bring your feet close together. Do not slide your feet either. If you take this step quickly it resembles a jump. Continue to tap dance during this lesson.

6. The offense then walks back toward the original position. Defense maintains the 3 yard separation. Repeat forcing right.

7. The offense now walks back and forth, not sideways, for about 30 seconds while the defense switches forcing left and then right about every 5 seconds.

Part 3

8. The offense continues to walk back and forth at will. Walk only—no jogging. Add faking. The defense must watch the offensive player's midsection rather than the limbs (or ball) to avoid being faked out.

9. The defense forces left for 20 seconds then right for 20 seconds.

Part 4

10. The offense jogs back and forth, not to the sides, at will.

11. Force left and right for 10-20 seconds. Maintain the 3 yard distance.

Part 5

12. The defense moves 1 yard from the offense. Continue.

Key Points

1. The defense toils for less than 30 seconds in each part. Make sure you force both left and right.

2. Players move in the half down position, jump stepping back and forth.

3. An assistant checks the distance and position of the defense relative to the offense.

4. The offense moves only up and back, not sideways.

4 Three Yard Lesson

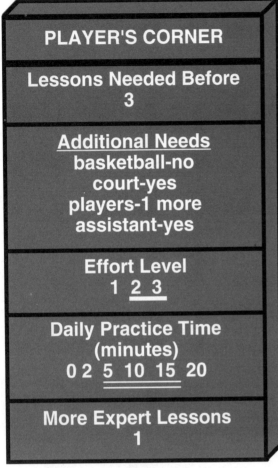

PLAYER'S CORNER

Lessons Needed Before
3

Additional Needs
basketball-no
court-yes
players-1 more
assistant-yes

Effort Level
1 <u>2</u> 3

Daily Practice Time
(minutes)
0 2 <u>5 10 15</u> 20

More Expert Lessons
1

Brief:

The defense stays a constant distance of three yards from the offense forcing them to dribble left or right.

Why Do This

The key to defensing a player with the ball is to stay a constant distance away. As the offense moves closer to the basket this distance decreases. Three yards is used for most lessons because at this distance it is easy to recover from a mistake. You can readily shorten this distance for tighter coverage when more expert.

The offense does not have a ball for several reasons. One, the offense can more easily maneuver without the ball. So this makes it more difficult for the defense. Two, the defense gets in the habit of looking at the offensive midsection, not the ball. Three, many offensive players do not dribble well enough to give the defense a work out. This could be used as a dribbling lesson if the offense were more expert.

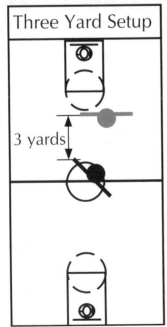

Three Yard Setup

3 yards

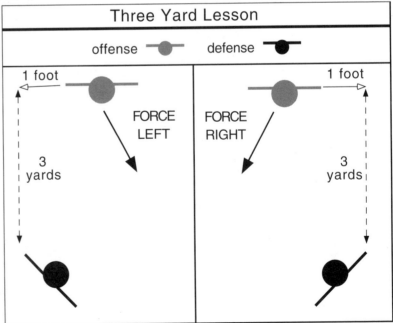

Three Yard Lesson

offense ⚫ defense ⚫

1 foot
FORCE LEFT
3 yards

FORCE RIGHT
1 foot
3 yards

Directions

1. Execute this lesson with 2 players on the court at one time. Time it for 25 seconds.

2. The offense can operate at full tilt if the defense is capable. Start out slowly, even walking, and gradually increase speed.

3. The offense not only moves back and forth but also left and right.

4. The defense maintains a distance of 3 yards from the offense. Watch the midsection of the offense.

5. Alternate forcing left and then right about every 5-10 seconds.

Key Points

1. Time this lesson for 25 seconds.

2. The offense speeds up as the defense becomes more expert.

3. The defense stays in the half down position on the balls of the feet jump stepping and running to stay in the force left or right position.

More Expert Lessons

Mirror Lesson

1. The offense lines up head to head with the defense. Move side to side only.

2. The defense attempts to stay in front of the offense. This is difficult.

3. Let the offense increase the speed as the defense becomes more expert.

4. To make this more fun, the defense can try to match offensive arm movements as well.

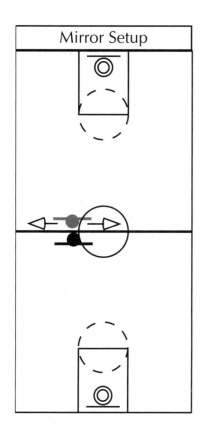

Mirror Setup

5 Trapping 1-3

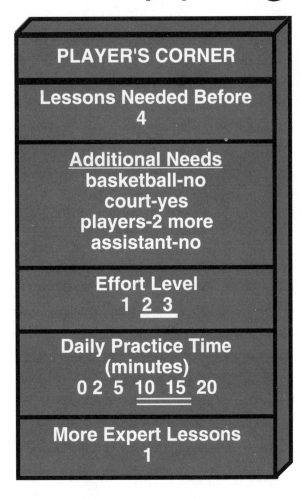

Brief:

Two defensive players prevent an offensive player from dribbling forward.

Why Do This

In both half and full court presses, trapping hampers an offensive player's effort to advance the ball. Trapping stops the dribble as well as hinders passing. Two defensive players normally trap one offensive player with the ball. However, a smart defensive player can use the sideline, instead of another player, to trap the offense. The usual trap involves one player forcing left while the other forces right. This lesson involves forcing, communication, hustle, and conditioning. Again the offense does not use a ball, so this lesson is difficult for the defense.

Directions

Part 1- Setup

1. The defensive players set up one yard away from the offense with their inside feet slightly inside the feet of the offense. The outside feet are both outside the feet of the offense and forward toward the offense. See the diagram. This positioning necessitates that the offense move backward.

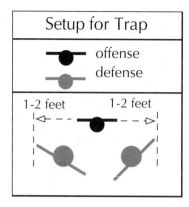

Setup for Trap

- offense
- defense

1-2 feet — 1-2 feet

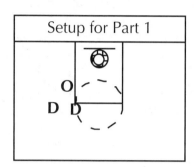

Setup for Part 1

O

D D

2. The offense tries to walk by, through, or around the defense. No running.

3. The defense prevents forward movement by keeping the offense in the same relative position between the two players. Coordinate your efforts. Block the offense if they try to go through or around.

4. Each play lasts 5-15 seconds.

5. Repeat until each player has been on offense at least twice.

Part 2- Speed Up

6. As the defense learns how to trap, speed up the offense. Go full speed using the entire court.

Key Points

1. Initially the defense blocks the offense. Then it only blocks for protection from a charge.

2. In a game the offensive player has a ball, so the defense keeps their arms extended outward and hands low to stop the dribbling.

3. Switch left and right trapping positions.

4. In a game always wait until the offense dribbles before trapping. You also want to trap close to the sidelines to reduce the passing lanes.

5. Advice to an offensive player–never dribble into a trap. Be patient, wait until you can pass the ball up court.

More Expert Lessons

Tying Up a Player

Once a player is trapped you need to prevent the pass and most importantly not foul. If the player holds the ball for 5 seconds, it is a jump. The tied up player may throw a bad pass that goes out of bounds or that is intercepted. If you can get your hands on the ball for a jump so much the better. Again, do not foul.

1. This is very much like a more expert part of Lesson 12, Pivot with Defense.

2. Two defensive players go after the ball of an offensive player. One starts on either side of the offense.

3. Do not flail your arms or even look like you are hacking the opponent. Be aggressive but patient. The offense only has 5 seconds. A foul defeats the purpose of the trap.

4. The offense can pivot and push the ball high-low, close-far, and left-right. No dribbling.

6 Front-Keep Out of Lane

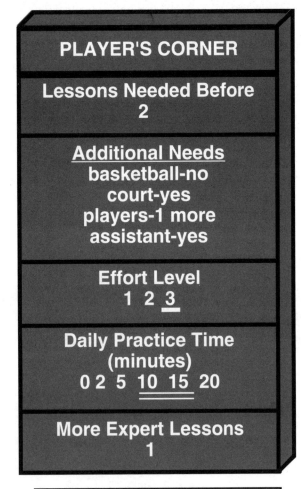

PLAYER'S CORNER

Lessons Needed Before
2

Additional Needs
basketball-no
court-yes
players-1 more
assistant-yes

Effort Level
1 2 <u>3</u>

Daily Practice Time
(minutes)
0 2 5 <u>10</u> <u>15</u> 20

More Expert Lessons
1

Defensive Movement in The Lane

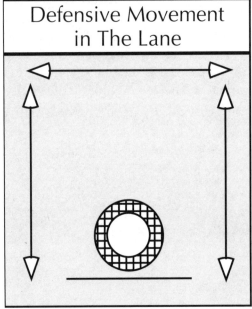

Brief:

The defense prevents the offense from entering the lane area by stepping in front and blocking.

Why Do This

Lessons 6-8 primarily teach how to cover a player without the ball. They also help with on ball coverage. Fronting means that you play the offense face-to-face without distraction. You do not look for the ball. The fronting skill has one major game application in out-of-bounds plays. This lesson, on the other hand, has several other defensive applications: one-on-one play, blocking, and boxing out. This lesson also reduces both the fear and fouling that occurs with more contact between players. Hustle is also involved.

Directions

1. The offense starts at the foul line. The defense starts in the half down position from within the lane and always faces the offense.

2. The offensive objective is to get past the defense into the lane. Initially, walk.

3. The defense blocks the offense with the arms and body. If the offense charges into the lane push them off with your hands. Push their upper arms and shoulders, rather than their stomach and face. Mom and dad will appreciate it. The offense initiates the contact if you are positioned properly.

4. Time the lesson for 10 seconds or the defense counts to 10.

Key Points

1. When fronting never look for the ball. Keep your eyes on the player's midsection (and eyes if you expect a pass).

2. The offense must work hard so that the defense gets practice.

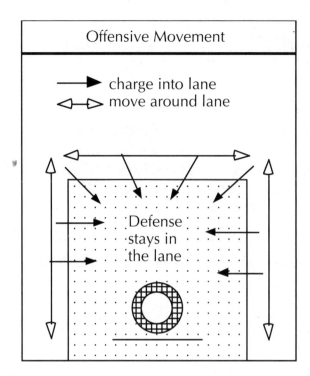

Offensive Movement

→ charge into lane
◁─▷ move around lane

Defense stays in the lane

3. The defense stays in the half down position, jump stepping around the lane.

More Expert Lessons

Front and Box Out

This is a continuation of the previous lesson. At the end of the lesson the defense shouts, "shot." At this point the offense goes straight for the basket. The defense blocks, pivots, and then boxes out the offense. You need lessons 13-14 before doing this one.

7 Overplay 1-6

PLAYER'S CORNER

Lessons Needed Before
4

Additional Needs
basketball-yes
court-yes
players-1 more
assistant-yes

Effort Level
1 2 **3**

Daily Practice Time
Part 1–10-15 minutes
Parts 2 to 5 –5-10 minutes

More Expert Lessons
0

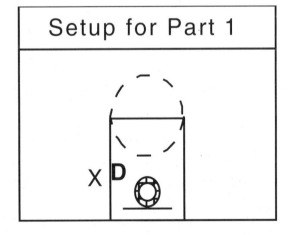

Setup for Part 1

Brief:

These 6 lessons teach defense away from the ball emphasizing coverage near the basket. Experienced players can do several parts in one day.

Part 1 introduces the body position and movements used in overplaying.

In Part 2 the defense prevents an offensive player from moving into the lane.

Part 3 involves a player cutting behind the defense.

In Part 4 boxing out is added to Part 3.

In Part 5 the defense covers the offense after losing contact.

Part 6 involves a player cutting in front from the high post.

Why Do This

These lessons are the key to both individual and team defense. Overplaying prevents the offense from catching a pass where they want– close to the basket. It also prevents cuts into the low post or any other area as well as curtails offensive rebounds–because it's easy to box out from the overplaying position. As a team skill overplaying facilitates strong-weak side help. These lessons are more important than defense *on the ball* because they teach defense *near the basket* where teams both shoot best and score the most points. Good defense alters this. Lessons 55 and 56 in The Player's Manual apply overplaying in a realistic situation.

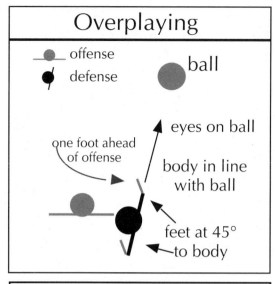

Overplaying

offense
defense
ball
eyes on ball
one foot ahead of offense
body in line with ball
feet at 45° to body

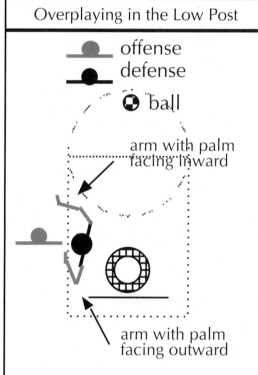

Overplaying in the Low Post

offense
defense
ball
arm with palm facing inward
arm with palm facing outward

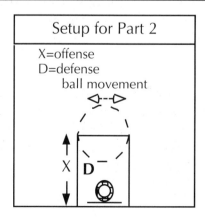

Setup for Part 2

X=offense
D=defense
ball movement
X   D

Directions

Part 1- Overplay

1. The offense starts in the low post. The defense sets up in the lane next to offense. Place the ball initially at the top of the key. As the ball position changes so does the defensive setup.

2. The defense faces the offense with one foot one step ahead. The right foot is ahead on the left side; the left on the right side. The behind foot is almost in a straight line with the other foot and the ball.

3. If you put your arms straight out, the front arm points forward downcourt, the other points toward the endline. Bend both elbows slightly downward. The palm of the front hand faces inward. The hand is in a ready position to deflect a pass. Rotate the back forearm and hand clockwise. Bend the wrist and the arm back so that the palm is facing toward the sidelines and the opponent. The hand is in position to touch the offense. Move it back and forth to sense offensive movement.

4. Move both arms toward the offense so that you are touching them. Touch them with your back hand and your front elbow. Feel where the offense moves. Offense– slowly move 2-3 steps up and down the lane.

5. Defense–keep your eyes on the ball while you do this. Move, so that you stay in the same position relative to the offense.

6. If the offense attempts to step in the lane in front of you they should bump into your forearm and body. Offense, try stepping in the lane.

7. If they attempt to step behind you into the lane they should bump into your back arm and body. Offense, try it.

8. Change sides of the lane and then repeat steps 1-7

Part 2- Prevent Movement into Lane

9. The offense attempts to go into the lane in the low post area, either behind or in front of the defense.

10. The defense jump steps forward and backward playing the offense by touch, preventing the penetration by contact with the body and arms.

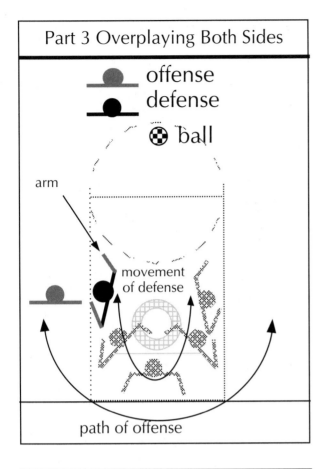

Part 3 Overplaying Both Sides

offense
defense
⊗ ball

arm

movement of defense

path of offense

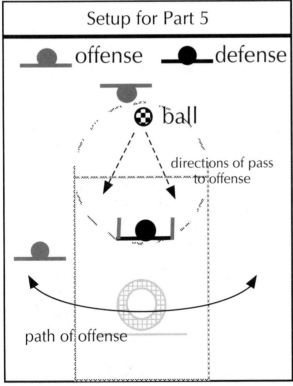

Setup for Part 5

offense   defense

⊗ ball

directions of pass to offense

path of offense

Keep your eyes on the ball, not on the defense, as you do this. Continue play for 10-20 seconds. The defense can count or estimate.

• Playing by touch means that you slightly move your arms to barely touch the offensive player. If you make this touch too obvious, the ref may call a foul.

11. Work on both sides of the lane. The offense speeds up as the defense catches on.

12. Go to Part 3 only when players can overplay with the offense at full speed.

Part 3- Overplay Both Sides

13. The offense first tries to cut in front and then goes behind the defense. Go to the other side of the lane behind the backboard.

14. Defense–prevent the offense from stepping into the lane. When the offense goes behind the backboard, not just behind you, allow the offense to cross over to the other side of the lane. Keep your eyes on the ball. Your body also faces the ball. See the diagram.

15. When the offense comes close to the basket, stay in contact using your arms and back; be more physical. Keep the offense on your back, boxed out. Continue to play the offense on the other side of the lane.

16. Run this part for 10-20 seconds.

Part 4- Overplay and Box Out

17. Boxing out is added to Part 3. See lessons 13 and 14.

18. After 3-6 seconds the defense yells, "shot." The offense then goes straight for the basket. The defense blocks and then boxes them out. This should be easy since the offense is on the back of the defense to begin with.

Part 5- No Touch D

19. This teaches players what to do if they lose the offense under the boards. A player at the top of the key attempts to pass the ball to the offensive player who starts one or two steps behind the defense on the lane.

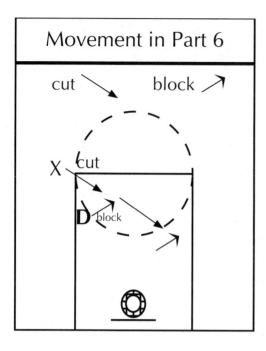

Movement in Part 6

cut ↘   block ↗

X cut

D block

20. The defense takes a position one foot in front of the basket in the center of the lane. Watch the ball only. You have lost contact with the offense.

21. Do not turn around to look for the offense. If you watch the passer, you will find that a pass cannot be thrown into the lane.

22. The passer tries to hit an open player in the lane. Pass the ball within 6 seconds. Count out loud.

In a game locate your coverage at the first opportune moment–when a pass will not be thrown into the lane.

Part 6- Overplay Cutter

23. The offense cuts from the high post on one side to the low post on the other side.

24. The defense stays ahead of the cutter. Prevent the cutter from making a straight cut by stopping in front. This contact, all across the lane, slows the cutter, making passes difficult to both time and throw. When 3-4 feet from the basket, stay in front of the cutter.

Key Points

1. The offense walks slowly at first. As the defense develops, increase the speed of the offense. You will learn defense better if the offense goes slower than faster.

2. The defense looks at the ball at all times. Play defense by touch.

3. Never let a player walk or cut into the lane without contact. You must virtually block any offensive player attempting to cut into the lane from the low post or basket or even from slightly behind the basket.

4. Block out after the shot.

8 Defense the Low Post 1-3

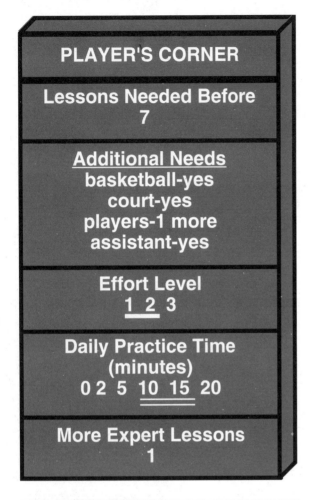

PLAYER'S CORNER

Lessons Needed Before
7

Additional Needs
basketball-yes
court-yes
players-1 more
assistant-yes

Effort Level
1 <u>2</u> 3

**Daily Practice Time
(minutes)**
0 2 5 <u>10 15</u> 20

More Expert Lessons
1

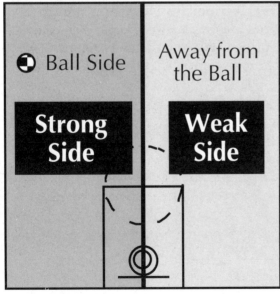

🕐 Ball Side

Away from
the Ball

**Strong
Side**

**Weak
Side**

Brief:

Part 1 covers defense in the low post, strong and weak side.

In Part 2 defense is played as the ball moves from one corner to the other.

Part 3 covers strong and weak side play outside the low post.

Why Do This

In Lesson 7, Overplaying 1-6, the ball remains in a fixed position. In this lesson, as in a game, defense is played while the ball moves from side to side. Ball (strong) side defense and defense away from the ball (weak side) are played differently. On the strong side, the same side of the court as the ball, the defense plays aggressively to prevent a pass to the low post. On the weak side, the side away from the ball, the defense stays in a position both to help out on defense as well as prevent a pass inside. Note that the strong and weak sides are separated by an imaginary line down the center of the lane to the basket. See the diagram. However, strong side often only means close to the ball, whereas weak side, far away from the ball. In either case, the defense stays close enough to box out after a shot. Be aware that offenses go right in games more than left. You need to practice on both sides of the lane.

Weak side players are not immediate scoring threats like those on the strong side. So you can rotate away from the offense toward the center of the court to help cover strong side players. This is called helping out. The further a weak side player is from the basket, the more the defense can help out by moving or cheating toward the center of the lane. Professional (NBA) rules attempt to curtail helping out, so that there is more scoring.

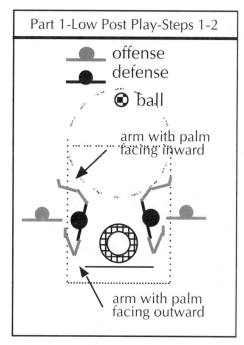

Part 1-Low Post Play-Steps 1-2

● offense
● defense
⊚ ball

arm with palm facing inward

arm with palm facing outward

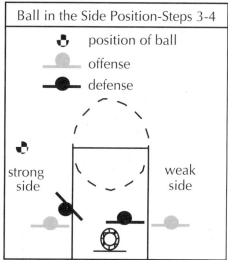

Ball in the Side Position-Steps 3-4

⚑ position of ball
● offense
● defense

strong side

weak side

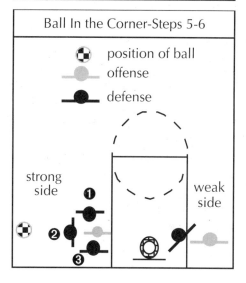

Ball In the Corner-Steps 5-6

⊛ position of ball
● offense
● defense

strong side

weak side

Note that defensive coverage of players farther from the basket is similar to the way you cover low post players. Of course you do not need to overplay as much.

Directions

Part 1 Strong and Weak Side

1. With the ball in the center position overplay the low post player like you did in Lesson 7, the previous lesson. This explanation is for players in either the right and left low post. The ball moves from the center position to the right corner. The directions going from the center to the left corner are identical.

2. In the half down position, shoulder to shoulder your body points to the ball. Your forward foot is slightly ahead of the offense; the back foot is slightly behind. Your eyes are on the ball. Again, play defense by touch as described in Lesson 7. See the diagram.

3. Move the ball to the right side of the foul line extended. The right side is now the strong side. Shoulder to shoulder strong side players point to the ball. See the diagram.

4. Weak side players pivot around on the back foot to squarely face the ball. This is called opening up to the ball. This is too open. It is difficult to prevent cuts and cover the offense this way. Rotate half way back to the original position. This is the half way opened up position we want. Shoulder to shoulder your body faces slightly to the center court side of the ball position.

5. Move the ball to the right corner position. Strong side players set up to overplay (Step 1) and then pivot on their front foot (right foot) to step in front of the offense with your back foot (Step 2). You are directly facing the ball. The inside arm is straight up; the outside arm is straight back. Often you can stay in this position till the ball comes out of the corner. If the ball is shot, squirm around the offense toward the inside hand that is straight back. If there is no shot, pivot on the back foot (the left foot) so that you overplay the offense from the basket side (Step 3). When the ball comes out of the corner move back the same way (unless the ball is on the other side of the court). Step in front with the back foot. Then step to the side, pivoting on the forward foot. See the diagram. Repeat this double pivot move several times.

6. Weak side players open up slightly more. Keep the offense on your back if possible.

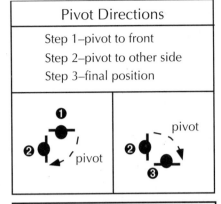

Pivot Directions

Step 1–pivot to front

Step 2–pivot to other side

Step 3–final position

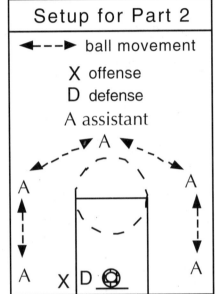

Setup for Part 2

◄ - - ► ball movement

X offense

D defense

A assistant

7. Move the ball to the left corner and repeat steps 5 and 6.

8. Do not stand so close to the defense that their body blocks you out. You need room to move for the ball.

Part 2 Move Ball Around

9. Have an assistant move the ball around the periphery while you are in the right low post and then the left low post defensive positions.

10. Start the ball at the center, move to the right corner, back to the center, to the left corner and then back to the center. Repeat this cycle twice, stopping to examine the defensive position.

11. Speed up the ball movement as the defense becomes more expert.

Part 3- Defense Farther from the Basket

11. Repeat steps 1 through 11 setting up farther from the basket. Use these positions (see the diagram) on both the left and right sides:

a. High post on lane–where lane and foul line meet

b. Foul line extended 3 yards–near the sideline

c. Corner–near where baseline and sideline meet

12. The diagrams show the helping out positions. When the defense is far from the basket and the ball, weak side players move directly into the center of the lane. The body of the defense directly faces midcourt and watches both the ball and the offensive assignment. This is better practiced with a team of players.

Key Points

1. The defense is in the half down defensive position throughout this lesson.

2. The eyes of the defense are always on the ball. The position of the offense is determined by touch.

3. Strong side players are aligned, shoulder to shoulder, with the ball.

4. Weak side players open up halfway to the ball.

5. Jump step and pivot between positions.

6. The forward palm is always facing the ball; the back palm is toward the offense.

7. Stand off the offense one foot so that their body does not box you out. You can also move toward the ball more easily this way.

8. Note that there are two ways to move around a player in

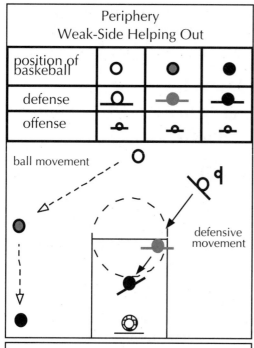

Periphery Weak-Side Helping Out			
position of baskeball	O	⊙	●
defense	⊖	⊖	⊖
offense	⊶	⊶	⊶

ball movement

defensive movement

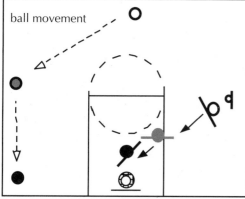

ball movement

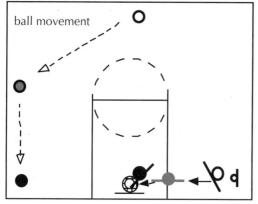

ball movement

the low post as the ball goes to the corner. One is to move in front as described in this lesson and the other is to move behind. Novices should always move in front of the offense. Don't worry about lobs. More experienced players can use whichever method works best for them.

9. In some situations the defense may be able to effectively overplay the offense from either side. The rule to apply in any situation is to use what works best. Learn one simple way, and then it is easy to adjust in game situations.

More Expert Lessons

With Passing and Driving

1. Instruct the assistant to attempt a pass to the low post as he or she walks around with the ball. Better yet, round up a group of players to pass the ball around the periphery, attempting to get the ball inside.

2. Move the defense to a periphery position. Tell a peripheral offensive player to drive to the basket every 5 or 10 seconds. If your defensive assignment is close to the lane, you cannot help out as much as a player whose assignment is far away from the basket. The defense, in any case, should move to the center of the lane in time to stop the drive.

9 D on Shooter

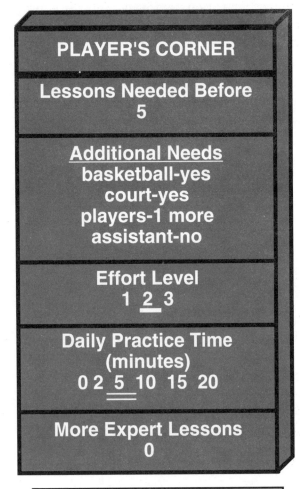

D on Shooter Setup

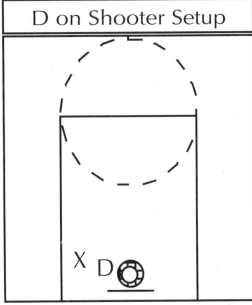

X D

Brief:
The defense harasses the shooter without committing a foul.

Why Do This

The key to covering a shooter effectively without fouling involves the movement of the arms. Any attempt to snuff the ball down the throat of the offense usually has adverse results. Often a foul is called, even if there is no contact, because the defense flails their arms. If there is a successful block, the offense usually picks the ball off the floor and then scores unopposed while the defense basks in the full glory of the snuff. The objective of the defense is to alter the shot of the offense and then box them out. This lesson shows many ways to alter the shot. Players practice boxing out as well. Players also practice offensive skills: shooting under pressure and going for the rebound after shooting.

Directions

1. The offense sets up one foot from the basket on the right side. Shoot any type of shot off the backboard.

2. The defense sets up right in front of the offense. The right arm and hand are fully extended upward, slightly to the right side of the shooter. If the shooter is left handed, the left arm is extended and slightly to the left of the shooter. Do not move this arm in any direction—side to side, back and forth. Especially, do not bring the arm downward to snuff the ball in the shooter's face. Excessive motion results in a foul call whether or not there is any contact. Let the offense shoot the ball into your hand.

3. The other hand should be about 6 inches or more from the face, or the eyes to be more exact. Attempt to obstruct the vision and distract the shooter. Wave your fingers; open and close your hand; any motion can distract the shooter. Your hand needs to be between the

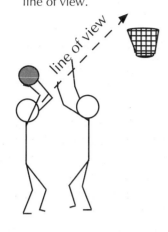

Position of Arms

The defense must place one hand in the offense's line of view.

line of view

eyes of the shooter and their vision of the basket. Shooters look slightly upward to shoot, so the hand needs to be slightly higher than the eyes, not at eye level.

4. Use your voice as well. Make funny noises. Yell, "fire, help, yikes, your laces are loose, your underwear is showing" or anything else that might distract the shooter. No abusive or derogatory statements concerning heritage.

5. Do not jump or make an excessive attempt to block the shot.

6. Repeat 5-10 times.

Key Points

1. The object is to alter the shot, not block it.

2. Players tend to swing their arms wildly to "put it in your face." To correct a slashing habit, repeat this lesson 10-15 times or more under close supervision.

3. Keep one arm straight up and the other in the vision of the shooter.

4. Adjust your straight arm for right and left handers. Be aware of this before the offense shoots.

5. Stand close but do not bump into the shooter's body.

More Expert Lessons

Shoot and Rebound

The shooter goes for the ball after the shot. The defense boxes out. Play whether or not the shot is made. Another option is to continue play until the shot is made. Whoever gets the rebound is on offense, the other player is on defense.

10 D on Driver

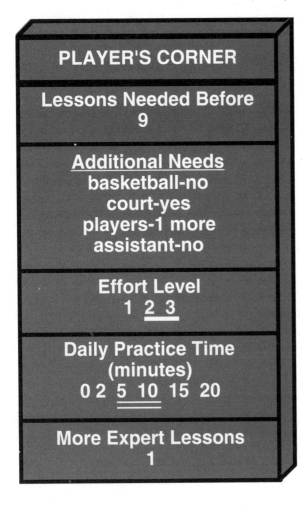

PLAYER'S CORNER

Lessons Needed Before
9

Additional Needs
basketball-no
court-yes
players-1 more
assistant-no

Effort Level
1 <u>2</u> 3

Daily Practice Time
(minutes)
0 2 <u>5 10</u> 15 20

More Expert Lessons
1

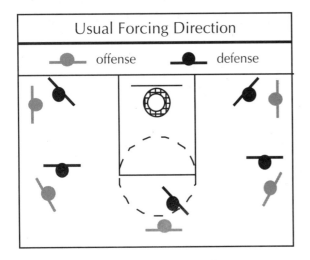

Usual Forcing Direction

offense   defense

Brief:
The defense covers a player driving to the basket.

Why Do This

The defense both sets up and covers a driver from many positions around the court. For several reasons the defense gets better practice if the driver does not have a ball. First the offense can move more quickly without the ball. This makes the defense work harder. Second, the defense focuses on stopping the body of the offense, not the ball. Focusing on the ball and ball fakes detracts greatly from a player's defensive effectiveness.

There always is a direction in which the defense wants to force an offensive player with the ball. In general you always want to force a player to go to his/her opposite hand side or toward defensive help. In the corner position you always want to take away the baseline because usually there is no help there. So, force to the center. Older players may want to use the baseline to trap a player. From the side position you again want to force toward help which is usually in the center. From straight on, you want to force to the player's opposite hand side. This is usually the left side.

Directions

1. The offense sets up without the ball in these positions- center, both sides, both baselines- and runs past the defense toward the basket. Start 5-7 yards from the basket.

2. The offense starts out slowly and then speeds up as the defense becomes more expert. Try to go in the direction opposite the force. Sometimes go straight to the basket. Use fakes as well.

3. The defense sets up 1 yard away or closer to the offense and forces them in the most favorable direction as explained below. Play is over when you stop the offense, or they bang into you, or they reach the basket.

Center of court around key

1. Force a player in the center part of the court near the key or foul line toward either the player's weak hand or toward defensive help. Force left in the lesson.

Side and corner

2. Force a player positioned on either side or corner to the center where there usually is defensive help. Never give a player the baseline since there is no help coming from out-of-bounds.

Key Points

1. Force toward help. This is usually toward the center of the court.

2. In the center position, force toward the left or the opposite hand.

3. Start 1 yard away from the defense and then close this distance as the distance to the basket decreases.

More Expert Lessons

2 on 1

Two offensive players start just outside the lane between the foul line and key. The player on the right has the ball. He/she dribbles in for the layup. Pass only if the defense stops you.

The defense starts in the middle of the lane. Force the dribbler to the outside. Make them pass. Most players have difficulty passing. Passing also slows down this break so that another defensive player can catch up. Have your inside hand ready to block the pass. After you stop the dribbler, fall back for the pass, shot or rebound.

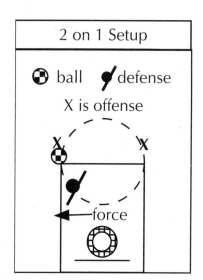

2 on 1 Setup

● ball defense

X is offense

force

11 Defensing the Pick 1-2

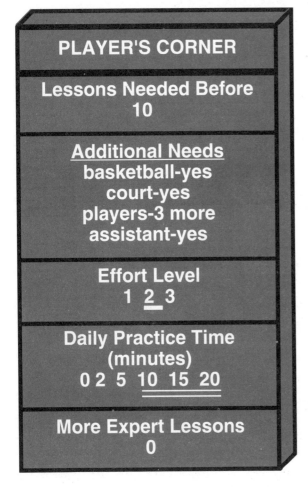

Defensing the Pick Setup

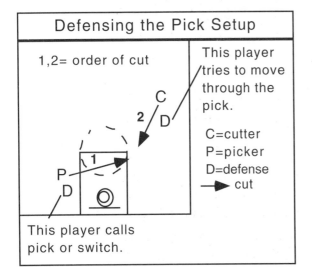

1,2= order of cut

This player tries to move through the pick.

C=cutter
P=picker
D=defense
→ cut

This player calls pick or switch.

Brief:
A player learns several ways to handle picks.

Why Do This

Picking is used to shake an offensive player loose from a tight defender, so it is more important for older players than for novices. Pros pick the most. Youngsters do not need this. Picks free up players to shoot, cut, dribble, and pass. Picking away from the ball is both more common and effective than picks on the ball because off ball defensive players are not as ready for it as on ball players.

The easiest way to handle a pick is to beat it. That is, slip between the pick and the offensive player you are covering. If you can't do this, then you need to communicate with the defender on the pick by yelling "switch." This means that you want them to cover your player and you will cover the pick. This can get tricky if the offense cuts back and forth behind the pick. Either defensive player can yell "switch" in a picking situation. Lots of communication and coordination is needed. If a defender is on his toes, he should call out any pick that he sees. For example, if a player sees a pick set on your right they need to yell, " Joe, pick on your right!" You tell them if you want to switch or not.

Directions

Part 1- Slip Through a Pick.

1. The pick and pick defense set up at the foul line (or anywhere else). A cutter sets up in the corner and runs toward the pick.

2. The defense on the pick needs to yell *pick left or pick right* as soon as they see what the cutter is up to.

3. The defense on the cutter needs to see the pick and beat the cutter to it. Just take one step behind the pick before the cutter gets there.

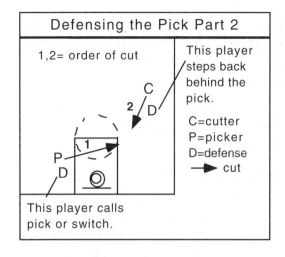

Defensing the Pick Part 2

1,2= order of cut

This player steps back behind the pick.

C=cutter
P=picker
D=defense
→ cut

This player calls pick or switch.

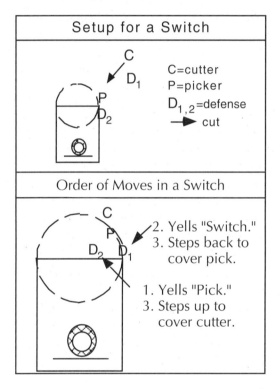

Setup for a Switch

C=cutter
P=picker
D₁,₂=defense
→ cut

Order of Moves in a Switch

2. Yells "Switch."
3. Steps back to cover pick.

1. Yells "Pick."
3. Steps up to cover cutter.

4. You can repeat this with the picker and cutter changing court position.

Part 2- Switch on a Pick.

1. In the same situation as Part 1 the cutter defense decides not to fight through the pick. Instead when the cutter is 1-2 yards away from the pick, the defense yells *switch*.

2. The defense on the cutter steps back closer to the basket to cover the pick. The defense on the pick steps to the far side of the pick to cover the cutter after they pass the pick. Often the defense can cut off the forward motion of the cutter if the defender on the pick jumps out to trap the cutter. This can be risky because it can put the defense in a worse situation.

3. Both players need to be ready to switch back if the offense gets tricky. This takes lots of communication and practice.

4. The offense should be tricky after players have more expertise. They should cut and pick for 20-30 seconds straight often cutting back and forth past a pick. Once in a while they should cut to the basket to see if the defense is on its toes.

Key Points

1. Only more experienced players need to bother with picks.

2. Both pick situations need to be practiced. Much coordination is needed for switches.

3. Beat or slip through a pick if you can.

4. Yell "switch" if you can't beat a pick.

5. Call out picks and where, left or right, they are as soon as you see one.

6. A few pointers for setting up picks:

    a. Set up in a direction to face the cutter.

    b. Do not move your arms or body for several seconds before contact. It is a good idea to fold your arms across your stomach or chest as protection.

    c. Take up as much space as possible.

    d. Be ready to cut to the basket if the defense is not on their toes.

12 Rebound Ready Position

Set up on a semicircle 8 feet from the basket.

The Ready Position

Brief:
Players stand with their body and hands ready to rebound.

Why Do This
When a ball rebounds it is difficult to determine exactly when it will bounce your way. Even after the rebound players often scramble on the floor for the ball. You need to be ready to catch or grab the ball at any moment. It may unexpectedly come right at your face. This is also the ready position for catching a pass.

Directions.
1. The ready position starts with the forearms bent up (or back) all the way.

2. The wrists are bent back and the fingers are spread and clawed.

3. The body is in the half down position.

4. Watch the shot and shot arc and try to predict where the ball will rebound. Move to the ball as soon as possible. It is okay to be wrong.

5. The assistant shoots from around the foul line. Some shots should be directly at you. It is okay if they are at the feet.

More Expert Lessons
Move to Rebound
Start in the ready position about 8 feet from the basket. Follow your prediction to the rebound. The objective is to get best position first. No need to jump for the rebound. It is better to do this with 2-4 players. The player in the best place gets the rebound; no fighting for the ball. Stay in the ready position throughout the lesson. Repeat 5-20 times.

13 Step in Front Box Out 1-2

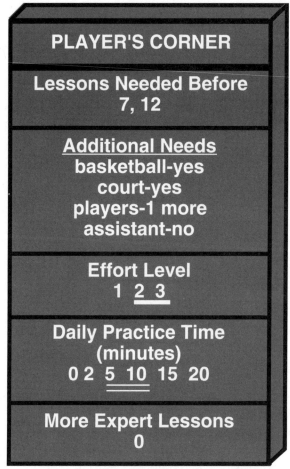

Setup

Starting Position

Brief:

Starting shoulder to shoulder two players work for the inside position.

Why Do This

Two players starting shoulder to shoulder work for the ball. Not only do you need to accurately predict where the ball goes, but you also need to step in front of your opponent. This is both an offense and defense skill.

To box out another player you need to keep him/her on your back. This impedes any movements. To get the ball the player needs to go around you. This is difficult to do quickly. If you keep another player boxed out for 2-3 seconds, you will probably end up with the ball.

Directions

Part 1– Step in Front

1. Two players start shoulder to shoulder 8 feet from the basket.

2. Start in the ready position and stay in it throughout the lesson.

3. Watch the shooter and the ball, not your opponent. Stay in contact with your opponent using your arms and body.

4. Step in front as you go for the ball.

5. The assistant shoots from different positions. Again, it should be no problem to miss the shots. Play made shots like a miss.

6. Change position on the 8 foot semicircle after each shot. Repeat 3-10 times.

Part 2– Box Out

7. Start from the same position 8 feet from the basket. This time one player is inside.

8. The inside player will keep the other player boxed out for 5 seconds by doing the following:

a. Spread the elbows out and back. Try to keep your opponent between your elbows.

b. To take up more space bend slightly lower than the half down position. Move your legs farther apart and stick your behind out.

9. The outside player initially cooperates by pushing gently on the back of the other player.

10. When the defense or opponent becomes more expert, the outside player attempts to get to the basket. Do not use finesse. Try to push around or through your opponent.

Key Points

1. Start shoulder to shoulder in the ready position.

2. Step in front as you go for the ball.

3. Watch and predict where the ball will go. Play your opponent by contact.

4. When boxing out a player, spread your body out by moving your legs and elbows apart.

5. Keep your opponent on your back between your elbows. Your behind needs to be out and back.

More Expert Lessons

Front and Box Out

Put **Parts 1 and 2** together. Start shoulder to shoulder 8 feet from the basket. Stop once you step in front of the offense and let them bang into your back. Take up a lot of space and try to keep your opponent on your back. To do this, spread your elbows apart and diagonally back. Stay in more than the half down position with the legs farther apart. Then go for the ball. Keep your eyes on the shooter and the ball arc. Play your opponent by touch.

14 Block Box Out 1-2

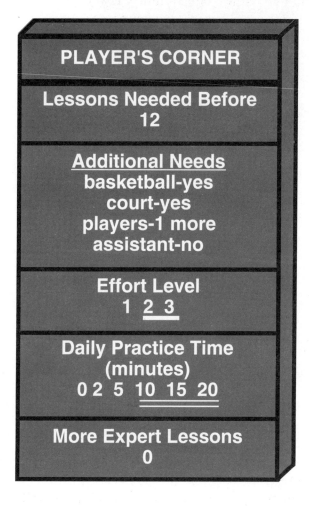

PLAYER'S CORNER

Lessons Needed Before
12

Additional Needs
basketball-yes
court-yes
players-1 more
assistant-no

Effort Level
1 **2 3**

Daily Practice Time
(minutes)
0 2 5 **10 15 20**

More Expert Lessons
0

Brief:
Players block offensive players charging for the basket and then box them out.

Why Do This
If a player is on your back to begin with, it is easy to box out. Getting them in this position is more difficult. A player running unimpeded to the basket for a rebound is nearly impossible to stop. Stopping the charge to the basket with a block is another key to boxing out.

Directions

Part 1- Stop and Box
1. The defense starts by overplaying the offense at one side of the foul line. Assume the ball is in the center of the court.

2. The offense charges down the outside of the lane toward the basket. Neither make tricky moves around nor charge through the defense. Initially run at half speed.

3. Five to eight feet from the basket the defense stops in front of the offense causing a collision. Use your arms initially to block the offense and protect yourself. As you become more expert make the blocking less overt.

4. After the block, pivot around whichever way (left or right) is easier to stay in contact with the offense. As you turn, one forearm should be on the offense. Keep the offense on your back between your elbows. This is boxing out.

Part 2- Shooting Added
5. Repeat this lesson with shooting and re-bounding. Make sure the defense overplays properly before the shot.

Block Box Out

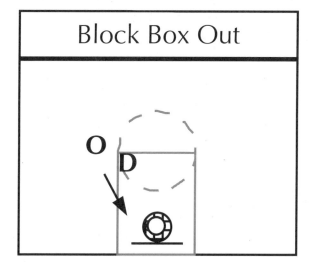

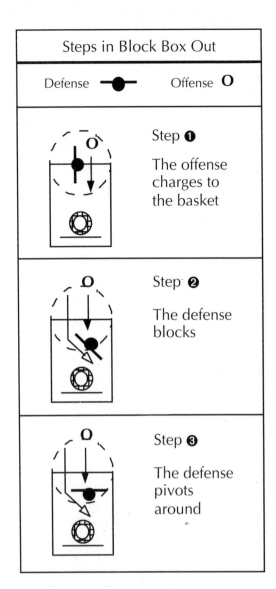

Steps in Block Box Out	
Defense ●—— Offense **O**	
Step ❶ The offense charges to the basket	
Step ❷ The defense blocks	
Step ❸ The defense pivots around	

Key Points

1. The defense rotates their hips and runs sideways toward the basket; do not tread backward.

2. At first, it is okay for the defense to be overly aggressive when blocking or boxing out.

3. The defense looks at the ball, not the offense, during this lesson.

4. After the block the defense keeps a forearm on the offense while pivoting around to box out.

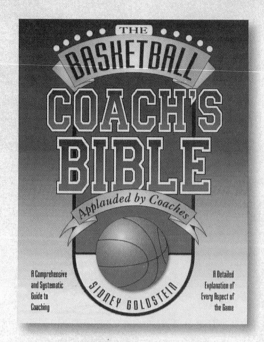

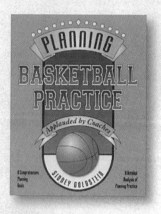

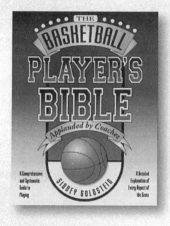

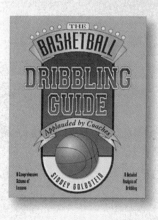
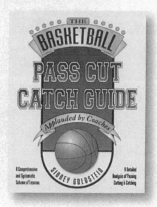
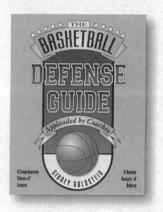

we've got videos and clinics

THE BASKETBALL COACH'S BIBLE WILL HELP YOU BY ...

- ✦ showing you how best to plan and run practice
- ✦ supplying two hundred field tested lessons ready to use
- ✦ systematically teaching each skill, step-by-step
- ✦ not skipping basic steps essential to your success
- ✦ presenting strategies, a warm down, game statistics and more
- ✦ saving you time by giving you methods and ideas that work

books

A. **The Basketball Coach's Bible**   350 pages
Everything about coaching. (07-5) $24.95

B. **The Basketball Player's Bible**   270 pages
All individual fundamentals. (13-X) $19.95

C. **The Basketball Shooting Guide** 45 pages
Yields permanent improvement. (14-8) $ 6.95

D. **The Basketball Scoring Guide**   47 pages
Teaches pro moves step-by-step. (15-6) $ 6.95

E. **The Basketball Dribbling Guide** 46 pages
Anyone can be a good dribbler. (16-4) $ 6.95

F. **The Basketball Defense Guide**   46 pages
Defense in every situation. (17-2) $ 6.95

G. **The Basketball Pass Cut Catch Guide** 47 pages
Be an effective team player. (18-0) $ 6.95

H. **Basketball Fundamentals**   46 pages
Covers all fundamentals. (08-3) $ 6.95

I. **Planning Basketball Practice**   46 pages
Use time effectively, plan, plus. (09-1) $ 6.95

J. **9 Book Series**, A - I (01-6)   ~$20 off $ 81.50 w/ship

K. **2 Book Bible Set**, A,B (20-2)   ~$5 off $ 46.13 w/ship

L. **7 Guide Set**, C - I (21-0)   ~ $5 off $ 49.50 w/ship

videos
40-60 MINUTES; $24.95 EACH
CHECK FOR AVAILABILITY

1. **Fundamentals I** Over 25 individual skill topics. (77-6)
2. **Fundamentals II** Team Skills, plays & pressure defense (90-3)
3. **Planning Practice I** Daily, weekly, and seasonal planning. (75-X)
4. **Planning Practice II** Get 5 times more out of practice. (76-8)
5. **Shooting I** Technique, Hook, Jump Shot & Layup (78-4)
6. **Shooting II** Foul Shooting, 3-Point Shooting, Driving (79-2)
7. **Shooting III** Shooting under pressure, Scoring Moves, Faking (80-6)
8. **Dribbling** Technique, Position, Protect Ball, Looking Up (81-4)
9. **Defense I** Position, Forcing, Trapping, On Shooter (84-9)
10. **Defense II** lane/Post, overplay, Front, Help, Strong-Weak (85-7)
11. **Passing I** Technique, Overhead, Bounce, Communication (82-2)
12. **Passing II** Cutting, Faking, Passing with Defense (83-0)
13. **Rebounding/Picking** Going for the Ball, Positioning, Boxing out (91-1)
14. **The Transition Game** from Foul Line, Center Jump & Plays (86-5)
15. **Team Offense** Offensive setup, Plays, Pliable Offense (87-3)
16. **Team Defense** Helping Out, Zone Shift, Half Court Trap (88-1)
17. **Full Court Pressure** Offense, Trapping Zone, Out-of-Bounds (89-X)

SIDNEY GOLDSTEIN, MR. BASKETBALL BASICS, TELLS YOU ABOUT HIS BOOKS

"This series is about fundamentals. It is a step back to the basics and a step forward to improved training methods. It is a place to start and to return again and again. No matter what your coaching level, age or sex the fundamentals do not change. You will reap great rewards by recognizing, practicing, and applying them to your situation. Visit our web site for 60 pages of information about our books, more comments from coaches, reviews, discounts, freebies, basketball articles, tips, videos, clinics, and more: I guarantee satisfaction."

clinics

VISIT OUR WEB SITE FOR DATE, TIME, AND LOCATION OF COACH AND PLAYER CLINICS:
www.mrbasketball.net

order form

QTY	ITEM	TITLE	PRICE

SHIPPING
$25 = $5; $50 = $5.75; $75 = $6.50
ADD $1 FOR HOME DELIVERY

DISCOUNTS 50-75% CALL OR CHECK www.mrbasketball.net

SUBTOTAL _____

ADD 7% SALES TAX IN PA _____

SHIPPING _____

TOTAL ORDER _____

ALL BOOKS ARE 8.5×11. ALL GUIDES COST 6.95; NEW EDITIONS COST $7.45 WHEN AVAILABLE. ALL VIDEOS COST $24.95 EACH AND RUN 45-60 MINUTES. ISBN 1-884357-(XX-X) SUFFIX IN PARENTHESIS

HOW TO ORDER
Call **1-800-979-8642**

Use our web site: **www.mrbasketball.net**

Fax PO's to: **215-438-4459**

Use your credit card, send a money order or PO to: **Golden Aura Publishing P.O. Box 41012 Phila., PA 19127-1012**

name _____

address _____

city _____ state _____ zip _____

phone _____

card # _____ exp _____ home zip ____